DOG TRAINING LOGBOOK

DOG TRAINING LOG

Session Details

Date	Time	Location
Handler	Dog's Name	
Weather	Temperature	Additional Notes

Training

Type Of Training

Objective

Notes

Reward Used	Rating ☆ ☆ ☆ ☆ ☆

Map Out Training

TRAINING SESSION NOTES & THOUGHTS

DOG TRAINING LOG

Session Details

Date	Time	Location
Handler	Dog's Name	
Weather	Temperature	Additional Notes

Training

Type Of Training

Objective

Notes

Reward Used	Rating ☆ ☆ ☆ ☆ ☆

Map Out Training

TRAINING SESSION NOTES & THOUGHTS

DOG TRAINING LOG

Session Details

Date	Time	Location
Handler	Dog's Name	
Weather	Temperature	Additional Notes

Training

Type Of Training

Objective

Notes

Reward Used	Rating	☆ ☆ ☆ ☆ ☆

Map Out Training

TRAINING SESSION NOTES & THOUGHTS

DOG TRAINING LOG

Session Details

Date	Time	Location
Handler	Dog's Name	
Weather	Temperature	Additional Notes

Training

Type Of Training

Objective

Notes

Reward Used	Rating ☆ ☆ ☆ ☆ ☆

Map Out Training

TRAINING SESSION NOTES & THOUGHTS

DOG TRAINING LOG

Session Details

Date	Time	Location
Handler	Dog's Name	
Weather	Temperature	Additional Notes

Training

Type Of Training

Objective

Notes

Reward Used	Rating ☆ ☆ ☆ ☆ ☆

Map Out Training

TRAINING SESSION NOTES & THOUGHTS

_____

_____

_____

_____

_____

_____

_____

_____

_____

_____

_____

_____

_____

_____

_____

_____

_____

_____

_____

_____

_____

DOG TRAINING LOG

Session Details

Date	Time	Location
Handler	Dog's Name	
Weather	Temperature	Additional Notes

Training

Type Of Training

Objective

Notes

Reward Used	Rating ☆ ☆ ☆ ☆ ☆

Map Out Training

TRAINING SESSION NOTES & THOUGHTS

_____

_____

_____

_____

_____

_____

_____

_____

_____

_____

_____

_____

_____

_____

_____

_____

_____

_____

_____

_____

DOG TRAINING LOG

Session Details

Date	Time	Location
Handler	Dog's Name	
Weather	Temperature	Additional Notes

Training

Type Of Training

Objective

Notes

Reward Used	Rating ☆ ☆ ☆ ☆ ☆

Map Out Training

TRAINING SESSION NOTES & THOUGHTS

_____

_____

_____

_____

_____

_____

_____

_____

_____

_____

_____

_____

_____

_____

_____

_____

_____

_____

_____

_____

DOG TRAINING LOG

Session Details

Date	Time	Location
Handler	Dog's Name	
Weather	Temperature	Additional Notes

Training

Type Of Training

Objective

Notes

Reward Used	Rating ☆ ☆ ☆ ☆ ☆

Map Out Training

TRAINING SESSION NOTES & THOUGHTS

DOG TRAINING LOG

Session Details

Date	Time	Location
Handler	Dog's Name	
Weather	Temperature	Additional Notes

Training

Type Of Training

Objective

Notes

Reward Used	Rating ☆ ☆ ☆ ☆ ☆

Map Out Training

TRAINING SESSION NOTES & THOUGHTS

_____

_____

_____

_____

_____

_____

_____

_____

_____

_____

_____

_____

_____

_____

_____

_____

_____

_____

DOG TRAINING LOG

Session Details

Date	Time	Location
Handler	Dog's Name	
Weather	Temperature	Additional Notes

Training

Type Of Training

Objective

Notes

Reward Used	Rating ☆ ☆ ☆ ☆ ☆

Map Out Training

TRAINING SESSION NOTES & THOUGHTS

DOG TRAINING LOG

Session Details

Date	Time	Location
Handler	Dog's Name	
Weather	Temperature	Additional Notes

Training

Type Of Training

Objective

Notes

Reward Used	Rating ☆ ☆ ☆ ☆ ☆

Map Out Training

TRAINING SESSION NOTES & THOUGHTS

DOG TRAINING LOG

Session Details

Date	Time	Location
Handler	Dog's Name	
Weather	Temperature	Additional Notes

Training

Type Of Training

Objective

Notes

Reward Used	Rating ☆ ☆ ☆ ☆ ☆

Map Out Training

TRAINING SESSION NOTES & THOUGHTS

_____

_____

_____

_____

_____

_____

_____

_____

_____

_____

_____

_____

_____

_____

_____

_____

_____

_____

_____

_____

DOG TRAINING LOG

Session Details

Date	Time	Location
Handler	Dog's Name	
Weather	Temperature	Additional Notes

Training

Type Of Training

Objective

Notes

Reward Used	Rating ☆ ☆ ☆ ☆ ☆

Map Out Training

TRAINING SESSION NOTES & THOUGHTS

DOG TRAINING LOG

Session Details

Date	Time	Location
Handler	Dog's Name	
Weather	Temperature	Additional Notes

Training

Type Of Training

Objective

Notes

Reward Used	Rating ☆ ☆ ☆ ☆ ☆

Map Out Training

TRAINING SESSION NOTES & THOUGHTS

DOG TRAINING LOG

Session Details

Date	Time	Location
Handler	Dog's Name	
Weather	Temperature	Additional Notes

Training

Type Of Training

Objective

Notes

Reward Used	Rating ☆ ☆ ☆ ☆ ☆

Map Out Training

TRAINING SESSION NOTES & THOUGHTS

DOG TRAINING LOG

Session Details

Date	Time	Location
Handler	Dog's Name	
Weather	Temperature	Additional Notes

Training

Type Of Training

Objective

Notes

Reward Used	Rating ☆ ☆ ☆ ☆ ☆

Map Out Training

TRAINING SESSION NOTES & THOUGHTS

DOG TRAINING LOG

Session Details

Date	Time	Location
Handler	Dog's Name	
Weather	Temperature	Additional Notes

Training

Type Of Training

Objective

Notes

Reward Used	Rating ☆ ☆ ☆ ☆ ☆

Map Out Training

TRAINING SESSION NOTES & THOUGHTS

DOG TRAINING LOG

Session Details

Date	Time	Location
Handler	Dog's Name	
Weather	Temperature	Additional Notes

Training

Type Of Training

Objective

Notes

Reward Used	Rating ☆ ☆ ☆ ☆ ☆

Map Out Training

TRAINING SESSION NOTES & THOUGHTS

DOG TRAINING LOG

Session Details

Date	Time	Location
Handler	Dog's Name	
Weather	Temperature	Additional Notes

Training

Type Of Training

Objective

Notes

Reward Used	Rating ☆ ☆ ☆ ☆ ☆

Map Out Training

TRAINING SESSION NOTES & THOUGHTS

_____

_____

_____

_____

_____

_____

_____

_____

_____

_____

_____

_____

_____

_____

_____

_____

_____

_____

_____

DOG TRAINING LOG

Session Details

Date	Time	Location
Handler	Dog's Name	
Weather	Temperature	Additional Notes

Training

Type Of Training

Objective

Notes

Reward Used	Rating ☆ ☆ ☆ ☆ ☆

Map Out Training

TRAINING SESSION NOTES & THOUGHTS

DOG TRAINING LOG

Session Details

Date	Time	Location
Handler	Dog's Name	
Weather	Temperature	Additional Notes

Training

Type Of Training

Objective

Notes

Reward Used	Rating ☆ ☆ ☆ ☆ ☆

Map Out Training

TRAINING SESSION NOTES & THOUGHTS

DOG TRAINING LOG

Session Details

Date	Time	Location
Handler	Dog's Name	
Weather	Temperature	Additional Notes

Training

Type Of Training

Objective

Notes

Reward Used	Rating ☆ ☆ ☆ ☆ ☆

Map Out Training

TRAINING SESSION NOTES & THOUGHTS

DOG TRAINING LOG

Session Details

Date	Time	Location
Handler	Dog's Name	
Weather	Temperature	Additional Notes

Training

Type Of Training

Objective

Notes

Reward Used	Rating ☆ ☆ ☆ ☆ ☆

Map Out Training

TRAINING SESSION NOTES & THOUGHTS

DOG TRAINING LOG

Session Details

Date	Time	Location
Handler	Dog's Name	
Weather	Temperature	Additional Notes

Training

Type Of Training

Objective

Notes

Reward Used	Rating ☆ ☆ ☆ ☆ ☆

Map Out Training

TRAINING SESSION NOTES & THOUGHTS

DOG TRAINING LOG

Session Details

Date	Time	Location
Handler	Dog's Name	
Weather	Temperature	Additional Notes

Training

Type Of Training

Objective

Notes

Reward Used	Rating ☆ ☆ ☆ ☆ ☆

Map Out Training

TRAINING SESSION NOTES & THOUGHTS

DOG TRAINING LOG

Session Details

Date	Time	Location
Handler	Dog's Name	
Weather	Temperature	Additional Notes

Training

Type Of Training

Objective

Notes

Reward Used	Rating ☆ ☆ ☆ ☆ ☆

Map Out Training

TRAINING SESSION NOTES & THOUGHTS

DOG TRAINING LOG

Session Details

Date	Time	Location
Handler	Dog's Name	
Weather	Temperature	Additional Notes

Training

Type Of Training

Objective

Notes

Reward Used	Rating ☆ ☆ ☆ ☆ ☆

Map Out Training

TRAINING SESSION NOTES & THOUGHTS

DOG TRAINING LOG

Session Details

Date	Time	Location
Handler	Dog's Name	
Weather	Temperature	Additional Notes

Training

Type Of Training

Objective

Notes

Reward Used	Rating ☆ ☆ ☆ ☆ ☆

Map Out Training

TRAINING SESSION NOTES & THOUGHTS

DOG TRAINING LOG

Session Details

Date	Time	Location
Handler	Dog's Name	
Weather	Temperature	Additional Notes

Training

Type Of Training

Objective

Notes

Reward Used	Rating ☆ ☆ ☆ ☆ ☆

Map Out Training

TRAINING SESSION NOTES & THOUGHTS

DOG TRAINING LOG

Session Details

Date	Time	Location
Handler	Dog's Name	
Weather	Temperature	Additional Notes

Training

Type Of Training

Objective

Notes

Reward Used	Rating ☆ ☆ ☆ ☆ ☆

Map Out Training

TRAINING SESSION NOTES & THOUGHTS

DOG TRAINING LOG

Session Details

Date	Time	Location
Handler	Dog's Name	
Weather	Temperature	Additional Notes

Training

Type Of Training

Objective

Notes

Reward Used	Rating ☆ ☆ ☆ ☆ ☆

Map Out Training

TRAINING SESSION NOTES & THOUGHTS

DOG TRAINING LOG

Session Details

Date	Time	Location
Handler	Dog's Name	
Weather	Temperature	Additional Notes

Training

Type Of Training

Objective

Notes

Reward Used	Rating ☆ ☆ ☆ ☆ ☆

Map Out Training

TRAINING SESSION NOTES & THOUGHTS

DOG TRAINING LOG

Session Details

Date	Time	Location
Handler	Dog's Name	
Weather	Temperature	Additional Notes

Training

Type Of Training

Objective

Notes

Reward Used	Rating ☆ ☆ ☆ ☆ ☆

Map Out Training

TRAINING SESSION NOTES & THOUGHTS

_____

_____

_____

_____

_____

_____

_____

_____

_____

_____

_____

_____

_____

_____

_____

_____

_____

_____

_____

DOG TRAINING LOG

Session Details

Date	Time	Location
Handler	Dog's Name	
Weather	Temperature	Additional Notes

Training

Type Of Training

Objective

Notes

Reward Used	Rating ☆ ☆ ☆ ☆ ☆

Map Out Training

TRAINING SESSION NOTES & THOUGHTS

DOG TRAINING LOG

Session Details

Date	Time	Location
Handler	Dog's Name	
Weather	Temperature	Additional Notes

Training

Type Of Training

Objective

Notes

Reward Used	Rating ☆ ☆ ☆ ☆ ☆

Map Out Training

TRAINING SESSION NOTES & THOUGHTS

_____

_____

_____

_____

_____

_____

_____

_____

_____

_____

_____

_____

_____

_____

_____

_____

_____

_____

_____

_____

DOG TRAINING LOG

Session Details

Date	Time	Location
Handler	Dog's Name	
Weather	Temperature	Additional Notes

Training

Type Of Training

Objective

Notes

Reward Used	Rating ☆ ☆ ☆ ☆ ☆

Map Out Training

TRAINING SESSION NOTES & THOUGHTS

DOG TRAINING LOG

Session Details

Date	Time	Location
Handler	Dog's Name	
Weather	Temperature	Additional Notes

Training

Type Of Training

Objective

Notes

Reward Used	Rating ☆ ☆ ☆ ☆ ☆

Map Out Training

TRAINING SESSION NOTES & THOUGHTS

_____

_____

_____

_____

_____

_____

_____

_____

_____

_____

_____

_____

_____

_____

_____

_____

_____

_____

_____

_____

DOG TRAINING LOG

Session Details

Date	Time	Location
Handler	Dog's Name	
Weather	Temperature	Additional Notes

Training

Type Of Training

Objective

Notes

Reward Used	Rating ☆ ☆ ☆ ☆ ☆

Map Out Training

TRAINING SESSION NOTES & THOUGHTS

DOG TRAINING LOG

Session Details

Date	Time	Location
Handler	Dog's Name	
Weather	Temperature	Additional Notes

Training

Type Of Training

Objective

Notes

Reward Used	Rating ☆ ☆ ☆ ☆ ☆

Map Out Training

TRAINING SESSION NOTES & THOUGHTS

DOG TRAINING LOG

Session Details

Date	Time	Location
Handler	Dog's Name	
Weather	Temperature	Additional Notes

Training

Type Of Training

Objective

Notes

Reward Used	Rating ☆ ☆ ☆ ☆ ☆

Map Out Training

TRAINING SESSION NOTES & THOUGHTS

DOG TRAINING LOG

Session Details

Date	Time	Location
Handler	Dog's Name	
Weather	Temperature	Additional Notes

Training

Type Of Training

Objective

Notes

Reward Used	Rating ☆ ☆ ☆ ☆ ☆

Map Out Training

TRAINING SESSION NOTES & THOUGHTS

DOG TRAINING LOG

Session Details

Date	Time	Location
Handler	Dog's Name	
Weather	Temperature	Additional Notes

Training

Type Of Training

Objective

Notes

Reward Used	Rating ☆ ☆ ☆ ☆ ☆

Map Out Training

TRAINING SESSION NOTES & THOUGHTS

DOG TRAINING LOG

Session Details

Date	Time	Location
Handler	Dog's Name	
Weather	Temperature	Additional Notes

Training

Type Of Training

Objective

Notes

Reward Used	Rating ☆ ☆ ☆ ☆ ☆

Map Out Training

TRAINING SESSION NOTES & THOUGHTS

DOG TRAINING LOG

Session Details

Date	Time	Location
Handler	Dog's Name	
Weather	Temperature	Additional Notes

Training

Type Of Training

Objective

Notes

Reward Used	Rating ☆ ☆ ☆ ☆ ☆

Map Out Training

TRAINING SESSION NOTES & THOUGHTS

DOG TRAINING LOG

Session Details

Date	Time	Location
Handler	Dog's Name	
Weather	Temperature	Additional Notes

Training

Type Of Training

Objective

Notes

Reward Used	Rating ☆ ☆ ☆ ☆ ☆

Map Out Training

TRAINING SESSION NOTES & THOUGHTS

_____

_____

_____

_____

_____

_____

_____

_____

_____

_____

_____

_____

_____

_____

_____

_____

_____

_____

DOG TRAINING LOG

Session Details

Date	Time	Location
Handler	Dog's Name	
Weather	Temperature	Additional Notes

Training

Type Of Training

Objective

Notes

Reward Used	Rating ☆ ☆ ☆ ☆ ☆

Map Out Training

TRAINING SESSION NOTES & THOUGHTS

DOG TRAINING LOG

Session Details

Date	Time	Location
Handler	Dog's Name	
Weather	Temperature	Additional Notes

Training

Type Of Training

Objective

Notes

Reward Used	Rating ☆ ☆ ☆ ☆ ☆

Map Out Training

TRAINING SESSION NOTES & THOUGHTS

DOG TRAINING LOG

Session Details

Date	Time	Location
Handler	Dog's Name	
Weather	Temperature	Additional Notes

Training

Type Of Training

Objective

Notes

Reward Used	Rating ☆ ☆ ☆ ☆ ☆

Map Out Training

TRAINING SESSION NOTES & THOUGHTS

DOG TRAINING LOG

Session Details

Date	Time	Location
Handler	Dog's Name	
Weather	Temperature	Additional Notes

Training

Type Of Training

Objective

Notes

Reward Used	Rating ☆ ☆ ☆ ☆ ☆

Map Out Training

TRAINING SESSION NOTES & THOUGHTS

DOG TRAINING LOG

Session Details

Date	Time	Location
Handler	Dog's Name	
Weather	Temperature	Additional Notes

Training

Type Of Training

Objective

Notes

Reward Used	Rating ☆ ☆ ☆ ☆ ☆

Map Out Training

TRAINING SESSION NOTES & THOUGHTS

DOG TRAINING LOG

Session Details

Date	Time	Location
Handler	Dog's Name	
Weather	Temperature	Additional Notes

Training

Type Of Training

Objective

Notes

Reward Used	Rating ☆ ☆ ☆ ☆ ☆

Map Out Training

TRAINING SESSION NOTES & THOUGHTS

DOG TRAINING LOG

Session Details

Date	Time	Location
Handler	Dog's Name	
Weather	Temperature	Additional Notes

Training

Type Of Training

Objective

Notes

Reward Used	Rating ☆ ☆ ☆ ☆ ☆

Map Out Training

TRAINING SESSION NOTES & THOUGHTS

DOG TRAINING LOG

Session Details

Date	Time	Location
Handler	Dog's Name	
Weather	Temperature	Additional Notes

Training

Type Of Training

Objective

Notes

Reward Used	Rating ☆ ☆ ☆ ☆ ☆

Map Out Training

TRAINING SESSION NOTES & THOUGHTS

_____

_____

_____

_____

_____

_____

_____

_____

_____

_____

_____

_____

_____

_____

_____

_____

_____

_____

DOG TRAINING LOG

Session Details

Date	Time	Location
Handler	Dog's Name	
Weather	Temperature	Additional Notes

Training

Type Of Training

Objective

Notes

Reward Used	Rating ☆ ☆ ☆ ☆ ☆

Map Out Training

TRAINING SESSION NOTES & THOUGHTS

DOG TRAINING LOG

Session Details

Date	Time	Location
Handler	Dog's Name	
Weather	Temperature	Additional Notes

Training

Type Of Training

Objective

Notes

Reward Used	Rating ☆ ☆ ☆ ☆ ☆

Map Out Training

Made in the USA
Las Vegas, NV
26 November 2024

12745799R00061